# RESILIENCE
## THE STORY OF AN
## *Extra*ORDINARY LITTLE BOY

### CLINTON C. PATTON, SR.
M.H.R., LPC

Published by
*Patton Behavioral Health*
Oklahoma City, Oklahoma


Bulk copies or group sales of this book are available by contacting prydllc@gmail.com or by calling (405) 534-8355.


FIRST EDITION PRINTED JUNE 2016
Printed in USA



*Patton Sr., Clinton*
Resilience: The Story of an Extraordinary Little Boy
First Edition.


Library of Congress Control Number: 2016907797
1. Abuse 2. Resilience 3. Healing 4. Spirituality 5. Love 6. Christianity 7. God

ISBN: 978-0-692-69555-5

# RESILIENCE

Dedicated to troubled children, adolescents,
and parents of troubled children and adolescents.
You can be successful.

"I believe in You."

Clinton C. Patton Sr.

# *Touching Lives...*

Clinton Patton is a stand up, humble and classic man who puts family first. He's a man who leads by example, never afraid to admit he's wrong, will receive constructive criticism and make changes accordingly. He's a great friend, father and mentor who has no problem raising the bar for those he comes in contact with. I admire Clinton Patton because he never allows me to settle for less, he gives me that extra push not only in words, but through actions as well. I thank God, for allowing our paths to cross, he's pulled me out of my comfort zone and I'm forever grateful for that. Continue to do good, allowing God to use you, and continue being that voice for the fatherless sons and women experiencing abuse who feel there's no hope or a way out... Keep allowing your light to shine in this dark world. I love you and I am very proud to call you my friend, brother and mentor.

**Tasha B.**

I have watched Clinton over the years do things that his heart desired without someone really guiding him. I always thought it had to be true resilience to do what your heart desires, to truly act out what you need and want for your life without proper guidance and encouragement. Not everyone is strong enough to bypass the defaults in their life and just do it! He did. He is truly intelligent and outgoing. This portion of him has always been an inspiration because everyone does not have that make up.

**Maya J.**

Clinton, my only and greatest brother in the world, has always been a man of stature. As a child, I can remember Clinton assuming the position of father figure in my life. He took care of me when there was no one else around. Clinton has always been a lover of people, but because of his many traumatic experiences he became much more than a lover he became A Prophet to those of us who suffer with adolescent children with mental and behavioral disabilities. His education and personal experiences have shaped him into one of the most renowned therapist I know! He's awesome! He knows the minds of children who have been traumatized and is anointed to help heal those wounds through the power of Christ that works in him. Clinton is not by far a perfect being, but he strives to be the best and because of this, what you read today can really help transform your train of thought. Allow him to help you, for what he has to give comes from a higher power. Clinton thank you for everything that you have done for me and for my children, now I pray that this book touches the lives that you so honestly seek to change.

**Love Always, Katrina Renee Patton, Your Baby Sister**

# Thank You

I just want to take the God-given time to give thanks.

**Dear God, I want to thank you for all the special people in my life:**

Clinton Cornelius Patton II (CJ), My Son
Stephanie Patton, My Mother
Bonita Hamilton, My Mother
Bertha Lee Patton, My Grandmother
The Late Leewillie Hamilton, My Grandfather
Clinton Lynn Hamilton Sr.,
Clinton Lynn Hamilton Jr.,
Katrina Patton
Ashley Hamilton
Camilla Hopkins
Charnisha Hopkins

**My Uncles:**

Calvin Patton
Earnest Patton Jr.
Larry Patton,
Charles Patton,
Eddie Patton,
Stanley Patton,
Rodney Patton Sr. ,
Lionel Hamilton,
The Late Ricky Hamilton,
Undrake Hamilton,
Lee Willie Hamilton Jr.
Lew Portis (Uncle Pumpkin)
Andrew Johnson,

**My Aunts:**

Maryann Baker,
Loretta Portis,
Annie Johnson,
Elvis Portis,

**My Extended Family:**

Grandpa John Beard
Dewayne Beard,
James Mitchell,
Robin Beard ,
Brinkley Beard,
Terelle Bush,
Coleman Bush,
Cedric Bush,
Jonathan Scott,
James Mitchell,
Jeremy Kemp,
Robert Gray,
Quintarus Gaines,
Johnnie Marshall,
Shava Echols,
Elizabeth Hooks ,
Andrea Walker ,
Pamela Roe,
Tonya Jones,
Nasley Garcia,
Donald Forrest,
Dr. Betty Joubert

Clinton C. Patton Sr.

### My Extended Family: Cousins, Nieces & Nephews

Syniah Wilburn,

Harmonie Patton,

Felix Jones Jr.

Dezia Allen,

Secario Hamilton,

### Additional Friends, Teachers & Classmates:

Kiantra Denton,

Elizabeth Hooks,

Chivonne Lawrence,

Pamela Roe,

Shiloh Bryant,

The White Family,

Mrs. Cynthia Johnson,

Roshea Warren

Maya Johnson,

Dr. Larry Ford,

Tameka Carter,

Kiana Traylor,

The Class of 1999,

Mrs. Dorothy Jernigan,

Mrs. Margaret Evans,

Thank you for everyone whom you have placed in my path through the trials and tribulations. All your children had a vital role in shaping me to be the man that I am today and for that I am humble and thankful for your mercy and grace.

**"Thank All of You for EVERYTHING, and I love you."**

I want to thank you for separating my parents because the separation caused me to gain a village and that village is my motivation to love and help our children to experience a village-so that we can let your will be done Lord, all I want to hear at the gates when I am no longer in this and of this world Lord and in your presence is "Job well done."

And last but not least, thank you Lord for placing Stephanie D. Moore in my path, the values that you have placed within her soul has given me the drive and motivation to complete this book in order to fulfill your will by saving lives through my mistakes. Amen.

## I can do all things through Christ who strengthens me.
## Philippians 4:13

# Foreword

Some scholars define giftedness as the ability to rebound. Often times, this reflected in the student that attends school, despite coming from a home wrought with domestic violence, drug abuse, and constant chaos. By providing healing opportunities for clientele, expert therapists are skilled in recognizing those small moments when the client demonstrates the ability to overcome. This is resilience... bounce back. We, throughout the course of our lifetimes, will face a number of threatening situations. We see our loved ones suffer and pass away. Some will be victims of abuse themselves. Others suffer from immense poverty and homelessness. While others are subject to oppression and acts of terror. Many of these are ordinary events. Yet one's ability to remain standing is beyond ordinary. It is extraordinary. It is a unique gift that allows an individual to supersede situations that for many others, diminish the capacity to thrive.

Clinton Patton Sr. has embraced the principle of resilience whole heartedly. It is incorporated into every aspect of his counseling practice, professional consultation, and motivational speaking. As we enter an era where more than half of adults will experience trauma at some point in their lifetime, the value of developing resilience is beyond measure. This book tells the story of a man who through a tumultuous childhood, a victim of unimaginable circumstances, was able to free himself from the stereotypical outcomes of a traumatized youth. Patton embraced his personal identity and built pride within himself, utilizing his gifts and talents. In this text he offers a blue print for any person who seeks to do the same.

*Tamika G. -C.*

TAMIKA G. CARTER
Advantage Counseling

Clinton C. Patton Sr.

RESILIENCE

# Prayer for Change

    Heavenly Father, I come to you today with an open heart and a humble mind. I need you to open our hearts Lord. I come in peace, I ask you to remove the defensive spirit Lord. You said that thou have not, because thou ask not. I am asking you today to wrap the hem of your garment around your child today so that he or she can accept the love of the stories within this book. Lord, I pray that you give them the courage to change Lord so that your will for their life will be done. I pray for clarity within the wisdom that you have bestowed into this book so that it may be utilized as a tool to love others, learn to love themselves, give them hope when there is no hope and give them faith when trials and tribulations of life become difficult. Help us Father for we know not what we do. Give them peace as the journey for change will pass through storms Lord, I want you to show them that you are the light and the truth Lord, I pray that you give them understanding Father, and for them to know that this book is all out of love because love is correction. I pray that each child, adolescent, their parents or parent, grandparents and the community as a whole can foster love and encourage change so that we can live the abundantly in Love. "Let your will be done."


    In the name of the Holy Ghost, the spirit of love, the spirit of correction, and our Father who art in heaven for the sake of peace.


    Amen

RESILIENCE

# Table of Contents

Clinton C. Patton Sr.

# Refusing to Let Go...

## A Day That Changed Everything

"There is no fear in love; but perfect love casts out fear, because fear involves torment. But he who fears has not been made perfect in love."

I John 4:18

One morning like many others, momma was headed for work. I ran downstairs to kiss her goodbye. She yelled, "OK baby I will see you when I get back and I love you!"

I replied, "OK momma I love you too." It was a difficult morning because I couldn't find any clothes to put on for school. My sister's father stayed home with us. No sooner had my momma walked out the door did I explain to him that I couldn't find anything to wear to school. He responded in a slurred voice dripping with the scent of alcohol "Get upstairs and find you some clothes."

A small anxiety began to creep in as I whispered, "I can't." I looked down at my feet as I headed slowly upstairs to do what I was told. With each step, my anxiety worsened.

Within minutes, the thud, thud, thud, thud of my sister's father's footsteps could be heard coming up the stairs. As I imagined him entering the bedroom I sat in, a shrieking ripping sound like an object had been torn off of something resounded and echoed in my ears... and its was coming up the stairs.

Only six years old, I looked up at his large dark image brooding in the doorway. Dangling from his large hand was a cord he ripped from our orange and white vacuum cleaner. It was wrapped around his hand, almost like a bandage, while he stumblingly sauntered and yelled at the top of his lungs, "I told your ass to find some fucking school clothes!"

An indescribable fear washed over me as I became more than afraid and realized I was in big trouble. The large looming man with angry red eyes, reeking of alcohol veered suddenly at me in a rage, arms swinging. Blow after blow, he struck me like a man fighting another man in a bar fight... over and over and over again.

The pain like lightning bolts rocked in waves over my body and the heat felt as though someone was tearing the flesh off of my skin. "Mommy! Mommy! I want my mommy!" I cried until my voice cracked and I could not scream anymore. Each hit pierced my 6-year old body, each blow getting harder and harder and harder and harder, I began to think to myself "Why is this man beating me like this?"

My young frail body grew weaker and weaker by each hit. I knew I had to do something or this man was literally going to beat me to death. With all the strength I could muster, I crawled under the bed and held on to the metal coil springs. Crying uncontrollably then silently, I waited in excruciating pain until my mother came home. It seemed like it took an eternity for her to arrive from work. I felt like this man had taken everything left inside me, my innocent belief that life would be the way is should be and the love of life I felt deep down in the pits of my soul, but I refused to let him take my spirit. That day I almost died.

My mother came home. She called my name and yelled, "Bring me a diaper for your sister." I slowly rolled from under the bed and immediately went to the bathroom. My urine was red filled with blood. I carefully walked down the stairs. My mother looked intently into my eyes and recognized that I had been seriously injured. She yelled, "What happened to my baby!" There were bruises all over my body, some of them were bleeding, many were like blisters and I could barely stand on my feet to walk. My uncle Stanley picked me up and put me into my mother's car. She rushed me to Timken Mercy hospital where I stayed for what I thought was forever.

While in the hospital, I remember having all kinds of IV's running through my veins. I was severely dehydrated and beaten. One day, I was featured on the local news channel. They were visiting the children's hospital. At the time, I was building some type of multi-colored toy that you have to put a marble in and you could watch the marble pass through each section of the toy. Being on television and playing in the learning center made me feel better.

After getting out of the hospital I had to face the man that abused me one more time... in court. The day before the trial the prosecutor and my mother took me into the courtroom where the trial was going to take place the next day to prep me for testimony. The prosecutor said "You don't have anything to worry about, all you have to do is tell us what happened to you. He is not going to hurt you." I replied, "I know he hurt me bad." I spoke in a sad and light voice barely above a whisper. As I walked into the courtroom, I was terrified. Initially, because I saw everyone gazing at me with looks that pierced my soul, but additionally because it was very quiet except for the court reporter. You could hear each stroke of each key that she pressed.

At that critical moment, I felt so alone but knew I had to show courage. I began to think to myself, "I can do this, I am not afraid." So then I looked up and stared intently at this powerful figure in the black robe. I began to walk towards the witness stand, but I was too small to look over the stand so they had to place phone books on the seat for me. I was asked to place my right hand on the Bible, raise my left hand and promise to God, to tell the truth, and nothing but the truth. I replied, "I do."I then slowly climbed up onto the phone books, sat straight up, took a deep breath and waited on the first question. The district attorney stated, "Is the person who hurt you in this courtroom?"And I quickly replied, "Yes" and pointed at my sister's father. I began to tell the gruesome story of the morning I lost my innocence. Court began to feel like a movie and everyone was watching. As I told my story, you could see the faces in the courtroom transform with looks of disbelief, anger, sadness and almost everyone in the courtroom was crying.

At that moment I began to release the feelings of guilt because I didn't want to get anyone into trouble, but I also knew that it could happen to someone else and I did not want my sister to suffer the same fate. With confidence, I told the truth and nothing but the truth. My life was changed forever.

# RESILIENCE

I Believe in Me.

Clinton C. Patton Sr.

# The Color is Red.

"Whoever loves instruction loves knowledge, but he who hates correction is stupid."

Proverbs 12:1

Now we move on into my life between the ages of 6 and 13. I, who almost died when beaten at the age of 6 became increasingly angry. I realized that my father was absent. I asked myself, "What is wrong with me... where is my daddy?" Every time I thought about it, I became angry and aggressive.

I then turned to a life of gang violence. I wanted to make people feel the same pain I felt, so I began to fight and fight and fight as if there was no tomorrow. One day, I went to Mike's Discount Food Store with two of my cousins and as we were leaving some of our gang members approached. "Man we need to go in there and beat him up for messing with my sister." I replied, "Hell yeah! Let's go get his ass!" Then they went back inside the store to find the dude, they found him and next thing I know is that the dude tried to jump over the food freezer then "Pow!" The shot came from a .38 specialty. Dude began to grasp for air as he staggered to the front of the store, then another of the gang members reached into his pocket and stabbed the dude 3 times in his back. He fell lifeless in the middle of the floor with his eyes open and blood everywhere. I was in shock and utter disbelief, all I wanted to do was fight and instead, I watched someone die. The look on that dudes face continued to pop up into my mind repeatedly, I became worried that something like that could happen

17

to me. I ran out of the store as fast as I could. By the time I made it home it was on the news. I told my mother, "I was just there!" But I did not tell her why I was in the store.

I thought to myself, 'I wonder if I am going to make it to 21 years old?' Then exactly one week later, I was fighting and someone pulled a .25, put it in my face. Then he pulled the trigger. But the gun jammed. That day I saw my life flash before my eyes. I began fighting like my back was against the wall. It was at that point I realized - it was time for a change.

After that I went to Chicago for the summer, little did I know that trouble would follow me. It was me, my cousins Omar and John. My cousin John and I would fight the other kids in the neighborhood all the time. My first fight in Chicago was over a 'Michael Jordan' shirt. From that point on, I fought every day. John and I had been shot at several times, I began to think that we wouldn't live to see 21 years old because we didn't know how to stop fighting. We enjoyed inflicting pain on other people.

I was very easily agitated. I would fight at the drop of a dime and did I mention that I didn't win all of my fights. One day as I was walking home from school, I was approached by 3 kids around the same age. They said, "What set you claim." I replied, "The set that you don't like, what do you want to do about it?" A fight happened, all 3 of those kids jumped me, but I wasn't going down without a fight. That was a fight I lost, my lip was busted, my jaw was hurting and my body was sore. Those boys whooped me pretty good, but that didn't stop me from continuing my destructive behavior. In fact, it made me angrier than ever.

I had trouble in society and home wasn't all that great either. One night, I was asleep in my room and I heard arguing outside in the yard. I went to my sister's room and told her to stay there, then I went outside. As soon as I stepped off of the porch, I saw my mother fighting with her husband at that time... behind a gray Chevy Nova. He swung at my mother, violently striking her in the mouth, she fell on the ground screaming "Stop!" He stood over her as if he had conquered his victim, I ran outside to get in between my mother and her husband. He stopped hitting her and she got up walked to the front porch. She sat on the couch looking as if she was in the fight of her life, her lip was busted and bleeding. I hugged my mother in disbelief that someone who appears to be a man could hurt her. I witnessed several incidents of domestic violence. I saw my mother called names, threatened and belittled by the men who were supposed to love her.

I began to wonder if love meant that you had to hurt a woman. It was a pattern in my mother's life to invite men that refused to respect her. The words of those men rang loudly in my mind, they would say things to my mother like "Bitch, I will kill you, fuck your family, you just actin' like a whore, fuck you, I hate your ass, nobody loves your stankin' ass."

I was severely traumatized but I tried to act as if it didn't bother me, when deep down inside I lost a lot of respect for my mother and for other women because I saw my mother allow a man to treat her like trash and hurt her repeatedly. Instead of fleeing, she continued to cater to him as if nothing happened, but she didn't realize that all the while she was allowing me to be traumatized over and over again. I began to believe that my mother would be willing to put any man before her kids... as a result, I became rebellious. The pain that was caused by the men I felt like my mother was taking out on me. She drank a lot of alcohol. When she would drink she was extremely mean, she would say whatever she wanted to say to hurt anyone in her path and it felt like I was always in her path. She made it very difficult for me to love her because she used her words to tear me down. My mother took her pain and hurt, that the guys she chose to enter into relationships with, out on me.

I began to feel like my mother didn't know what it meant to love and that she hated me. I began to question my existence, in fact I asked God, "Why would you give me a mean woman for a momma Lord?" And the sad thing is, I really thought that the way she talked to me even though she provided my basic necessities was love.

However, in my eyes, my mother could do no wrong. I will defend her until the end of time, even though her choice of words caused resentful feelings.

RESILIENCE

I Believe in Me.

Clinton C. Patton Sr.

# Odds are Against Me

"Change begins with the individual who perceives the need for change."

Clinton C. Patton Sr. MHR, LPC

I lived with my mother and sister. I am the oldest of two children conceived by my mother. I lived in an environment consumed with alcoholism. My mother would drink a lot, and when she became drunk she would become loud and emotionally abusive. The sad thing is that my mother didn't believe that she was an alcoholic. My mother would call me names, names that mothers aren't supposed to call their sons. One day I didn't complete my chores the way my mother wanted and she had been drinking, she shouted "Bitch, call your daddy if you don't like the rules in my house." She would say things like 'You are the sorriest son I know, I wish I never had you, I don't know how I raised a son like you, you are stupid, I wish someone would shoot you in the head and I hope you die and I am not coming to the funeral' and the list goes on. I had to endure years of belittling from the one woman I loved in my life, my mother.

I began to think that I couldn't do anything right and that I was a failure. My mother made my sister and I feel terrible about ourselves. It was like my mother used her words in an attempt to make me weak, but the truth is she was doing what she was accustomed to. She made me question my existence and I even contemplated what would the world be without me. My mother's words were not encouraging. In fact, her words pierced my

Clinton C. Patton Sr.

soul. Little did she know, she was motivating me through pain to sever our relationship. I felt that it was too painful to maintain a relationship with my mother and she felt justified in cursing me out over any little thing. It started to feel like she was looking for a reason to curse at me and to call me names other than the name she placed on my birth certificate. I began to question my mother's love for me.

When I was in high school I would get in trouble in class for making fun of others. While the teacher was trying to teach; I was playing and very disruptive. I took everything as a joke. Although I was very strong minded, I worked hard to cover a lot of anger that was caused by pain. See, people didn't know that I laughed and played so much because I was trying to keep from crying. I was experiencing self-doubt. I thought that I wasn't as smart as the other kids. To keep the attention off of me, I would crack jokes on my classmates without remorse. I was very disrespectful toward my teachers and often refused to complete my assignment... regardless of how many times I was punished, I didn't care.

I attempted to turn my aggression towards football and track. There was an incident at football practice that I will never forget. One day after school at football practice, I began to run the drills, but I had pulled my groin earlier while playing basketball, so I wasn't able to run full speed. My coach became agitated with me and stated, "I don't see a start to your career." I was in shock that the man that I looked up to did not believe in me. I began to doubt my ability. I thought to myself that 'Maybe football isn't for me'. But I knew deep down inside that I loved to play and not only did I love to play but I was good at it. I had to realize that in small towns if the coach has coached a family member of a prominent family, then they are the hometown favorite regardless of talent or skill level and regardless of how many games the team lost. It was then that I realized that I would face additional situations where I would be doubted.

I didn't think before I acted, I acted directly off of impulse. I didn't care about the consequences of my actions. I had a victim mentality, I blamed my teachers for my bad grades even though I displayed absolutely no effort. I blamed my abuse for my explosive anger temper tantrums. I refused to take responsibility for my behavior, it was always someone else's fault... or because I was abused at 6 years old. I spent a lot of time living in the past. I would argue with any adult because I did not like to follow the rules and was not afraid of anything. I was very disrespectful towards female teachers because I was extremely angry, well I was actually disappointed because I wanted to feel loved by my mother and she chose to drink instead of showing me unconditional love.

I then graduated from Simmons High School and had my dreams set on college. However, in the time between high school and my sophomore year of college a series of unfortunate events began to unfold. I would again face tragedy in my life.

On September 9, 2002, my favorite uncle (Stanley Patton) was murdered, he was shot 8 times right in front of my grandmother's house. The people around the town began to talk about what happened before he was shot. They started saying that it was a drug deal that went wrong, they said, "Stanley bought some crack from the boy who killed him and the boy sold Stanley some fake crack." When Stanley confronted the boy it ended in a confrontation, Stanley put the boy in a sleeper hold and the boy went to sleep. Then Stanley went home as if nothing had happened. As he walked out of the house and stepped into the street shots rang out. He was shot 5 times in the face and 3 times in his torso.

His lifeless body lay in the street riddled with bullets. My mother made it to the scene before the paramedics. She said, "I knew he was gone when they picked him up off of the ground, he waved his hand and that was it."

I became furious all over again. I had to lock myself in my dorm room because I was afraid that I would hurt someone. I had to call my mother. She said in a very sad and tearful voice, "Son your uncle is dead, they killed my brother." I became angrier because of the pain it had caused my mother.

Regardless of my uncle's lifestyle, I loved him. I learned to cut hair because my uncle would allow me to practice on his head and shave his beard. While shaving his beard my uncle would say, "Make sure you get the little hairs under my neck," and I laughed and said "Ok Uncle Stanley."

Hollandale became different because my uncle would sing as he walked around the town. Traditionally, everyone could hear him coming before they could see him. The citizens around town called him R. Kelly or Maxwell because depending on the day he would sing

RESILIENCE

I Believe in Me.

either one of their songs and loudly.

Before my uncle died, I was talking to another one of my uncles and said "Our family don't come together for things like a family reunion, but if it was a funeral then they would rush home. I don't like that." To make matters worst, I was unable to attend my uncle's funeral.

On the bright side, I developed a meaningful relationship that evolved and eventually produced a gift I could never imagine—my son. I was proud to become a father.

Six months after my son was born, I received the most dreadful phone call. Yet again, I would face what I would say was "unthinkable." I decided that I wanted to visit my family in Garland Texas. I talked to my sister and she said, "Hey brother, I want to see you at dad's house." I replied, "I want to see you too sister, I hope you can make it down here. I am bringing CJ so you can see him." I then made it to Garland, Texas; it was August 11th, 2007 when we went to my uncle house for a pre-graduation party for his cousin. The family was having a good time, they were saying how much my son and my sister's son look so much alike. Then the phone rang and it was Ashley my sister. I grabbed the phone and said, "Hey sister, I thought that you was coming down here? I was looking forward to seeing my little sister." She replied, "Hey brother what are you doing? I had to work that's why I couldn't come." I said, "Ok, well what you doin' now?" She replied, "Nothing, I just got off work and I am tired. I am about to go to sleep." I replied, "Ok sister call me when you get up." She replied, "Ok brother," and that was the end of the conversation.

August the 12th, 2007, I received a phone call at about 4:00 a.m. The person on the phone asked, "What is your relation to Ashley Hamilton?" My sister gave the phone to Ashley's mother. The person on the phone then asked, "Are you the parents of Ashley Hamilton?" My sister's mother replied a hesitant "Yes, I am." The person responded, "I am a detective from the Jackson Police Department. There has been a tragedy, Ashley Hamilton was found dead from a gunshot wound to her head." On the phone, there was dead silence.

The following morning, I was awakened by crying and sorrow. I asked, "What are ya'll crying for?" My sister's mother replied "That boy killed your sister! I told her to leave him alone!" I said "What! You mean to tell me my sister is dead and not hurt?" The pain of loss started all over again.

I called his sisters cell phone over and over and over again... but there was no answer, and the voicemail kept saying "The cellular south customer is not available". I could feel the anger compound and become unconsolable as I exploded with passion, "Why did he kill my sister?"

My mother raised me to protect my sisters and brothers. My sister was murder by her boyfriend. Apparently, she experienced domestic violence for approximately 2 years without telling me. She lived in Mississippi. There was no way I could sense that she was going through something like that.

After she was murdered, I felt an enormous amount of guilt because I could not protect my sister. All of my life I was taught to protect my sister and I failed to do so and she was murdered. Gone. I couldn't believe that someone had taken her life, she was only 22 years old. She had two children. I would talk with my sister every day at the same time. When she was murdered that left a void in my heart, I couldn't sleep and I couldn't eat. My soul felt like a part of me was missing. We used to laugh and talk about everything.

Almost immediately after that, I began to have dreams about my sister. She came to me in one dream, she said "Big brother I don't know why he did this to me, I am sorry I didn't tell you about what I was going through," in a whispering voice, then she began to fade away and there was nothing there.

I decided to go back to work one week after it happened. It proved to be too soon, so I requested for more time off. I then went back to Mississippi to visit and to begin the healing process; while I was on his way down there something happened me. I began to daydream while driving. I envisioned a black and white house. I saw pieces of the door because it was kicked in. Then I saw a table with the double sink on the right side. I saw myself in the hallway reaching out for the gun but it was too late... her boyfriend shot her. Then I called my sister's mother and said, "You have the tub behind the bathroom door?" She replied, "No, but wait a minute it is one in the bathroom in my room." Then she told me that the detectives found my sister's clothes on the floor in the

RESILIENCE

I Believe in Me.

bathroom where the tub was behind the door. I said "Ashley was behind that door with the phone in her hand, she thought that he had left, but he didn't. When she opened the door and walked out he grabbed her by her hair and shot her."

Subsequently, one year had passed and it was time to go to court to represent my sister. I and our father made it to Jackson Mississippi that morning. It was nerve racking waiting to get the chance to see the coward who murdered my sister. They called the case number then my family and I walked into the courtroom and take a seat. A moment later, they bring the man that murdered my sister, the coward in a red jump suit, into the courtroom. Immediately, I was filled with anger, I wanted to rip the defendants head right off of his neck.

Then the prosecutor told my family that the defendant took a plea bargain for manslaughter to receive 20 years, a $10,000 dollar fine and anger management. A plea bargain is when a criminal accepts a lesser sentence if he or she pleads guilty to a crime. I became furious; I said to myself, "That was not justice served at all! When you kill somebody you should get life!" In my eyes, he lost a sister and this coward gets to live and that was a hard slap in the face. To top it off, he was released from prison after 8 years. For the next few years, I became a young man that would wake up angry and went to sleep angry. I felt like something was taken from me and it couldn't be replaced. I experienced several sleepless nights. I worried a lot. It was then that I transitioned into becoming a young man and realized that my anger was only hurting me. I, who became a young man, had to forgive as God had forgiven me for my transgressions even though it was murder. In order for God to forgive me, I had to forgive myself and forgive the person who took my sister's life.

Soon after, I called my other sister because I wanted to be there for her and avoid what could have been prevented for Ashley. One day, I received a phone call from my sister and in her voice, I could tell that something was wrong. She stated, "That boy jumped on me in front of all his people." I became furious, I thought "Nobody else will ever hurt my sister again!" I began to think of ways that I could go to Atlanta and beat up her husband. I talked to my sister's husband and stated "I have lost one sister and I will not lose another one, so I am telling you to keep your hands off of my sister."

I knew that I had to do something because all I could think about was being devastated that my sister was going through the same vicious cycle that left me to grieve the loss of my other sister. I took action. I decided to look up the police department in the precinct that she lived in and called them and asked them to do a welfare check on my sister. She was alone in Atlanta, in an abusive relationship and I feared for her life. The police went and checked on her. Only I knew because my sister called me and said, "The police just came by here," and I said "I know, I called them."

Soon after that, I was able to buy my sister a bus ticket and she was able to leave. And again, I found himself having to forgive another person for hurting my sister. I did because I knew that hating her husband wouldn't change the cycle of domestic violence.

## RESILIENCE
I Believe in Me.

Clinton C. Patton Sr.

# *End Domestic Violence*

Go checkout the documentary,
"Domestic Violence:
The Choice of Life and Death"
https://youtu.be/HsCyNbyyVeA

## "It Is Your Business."

Ashley Renea Hamilton

11/26/1984 - 08/12/2007

Clinton C. Patton Sr.

# The Transition

### I Became A Real Man.

A good man obtains favor from the LORD, but a man of wicked intentions he will condemn. A man is not established by wickedness, but the root of the righteous cannot be moved.

**Proverbs 12:2-3**

"Though I speak with the tongues of men and of angels, but have not love, I have become sounding brass or a clanging cymbal. And though I have the gift of prophecy, and understand all mysteries and all knowledge, and though I have all faith, so that I could remove mountains, but have not love, I am nothing. And though I bestow all my goods to feed the poor, and though I give my body to be burned, but have not love, it profits me nothing.

Love suffers long and is kind; love does not envy; love does not parade itself, is not puffed up; does not behave rudely, does not seek its own, is not provoked, thinks no evil; does not rejoice in iniquity, but rejoices in the truth; bears all things, believes all things, hopes all things, endures all things.

Love never fails. But whether there are prophecies, they will fail; whether there are tongues, they will cease; whether there is knowledge, it will vanish away. For we know in part and we prophesy in part. But when that which is perfect has come, then that which is in part will be done away.

When I was a child, I spoke as a child, I

understood as a child, I thought as a child; but when I became a man, I put away childish things. For now we see in a mirror, dimly, but then face to face. Now I know in part, but then I shall know just as I also am known.

And now abide faith, hope, love, these three;
but the greatest of these is love.
**Corinthians 13 : 1-13**

When my father and my mother forsake me,
Then the Lord will take care of me.
**Psalms 27:10**

As I continued to strive to be the best man that I can be, I needed to take a glance back at the beginning of my painful memories in order to get a better understanding of who I was. How did I get the ambition to succeed despite everything that has been against me? I must say, that it is the most horrible feeling in the world to have the one person who gave birth to you belittle you and display condescending behavior towards you. As a child, alcoholism destroyed my relationships with my mother. In fact, it was alcoholism that may have contributed to that dreadful morning when I almost lost my life at the hands of a guy who appeared to be a man when I was most vulnerable. I had to understand that my mother was a young mother. It seems like we grew up together. However, that does not make it right for her to speak to me in a rude and disrespectful manner.

Mothers are the first women that children learn to respect. I learned most of her actions and the words were not consistent, she would cook a meal but call me names at the same time. Unfortunately, my mother caused me to be confused. I thought that it was normal for a man to take verbal assaults. I thought that a man was supposed to show love by yelling and cursing at the top of his lungs to prove his point. My mind and heart experienced conflicted because I thought that abuse was normal, but in my heart, I knew that it was inhumane. As a child, you are taught that as a young man you are not supposed to let a female's words get to you. But in reality, those words cause heartbreaking pain deep within the pits of your soul. I have to be honest, my mother's words scared me as a child. She said words to me that I feel no mother should ever let cross her mind as it pertains to her children. Unfortunately, my mother taught me indirectly and directly through her interactions with men and myself that a woman can really damage a young child's self-esteem. I didn't understand her parenting style because I assumed that whatever her parenting style was caused more pain and I knew that it wasn't out of love. All this time, I've been searching for the love of a mother. I have longed for my mother's approval. Eventually, when I knew that alcoholism had taken over my mother, I turned to God to show me how to love, what love is, and what love looks like. As I grew older, more mature, and grounded in the word of God, I began to understand the actions of a man. All of a sudden, God told me, "Clinton you are love, I made you in love, it is easy for you to act in love because I made you in love."

It was then, after I received confirmation from God that I began to understand. Regardless of my childhood and the pain that I've endured by someone that was supposed to love me and care for me, my mother does not have the capacity to speak or display respect towards men. That may be a result of things that have transpired in her life as a young mother. I refuse to allow my mother's short comings to dictate what type of man I have become or serve as a representative of me..

Furthermore, I refuse to allow a society or environment, built for me to fail, force me to conform to its stereotypical behavior. It is my God given right to love and live an abundant life of happiness. To have the capacity to love... and most of all I love myself, no matter how much it hurts that I can't have a positive relationship with my mother. I still believe that one-day just maybe she will realize that she really hurt me, but until then I can have a wonderful relationship with God. He is the driving force behind my ambition to succeed.

**"Stop staring in your rearview mirror, the only time you should look in your rearview, is to switch lanes to move forward."**

Clinton C. Patton Sr. MHR, LPC

RESILIENCE

I Believe in Me.

Clinton C. Patton Sr.

# I Am Somebody

Train up a child in the way he should go, And when he is old he will not depart from it.

### Proverbs 22:6

During the times where I lived my life as that little boy, I realized that to everyone looking at me I appeared to be an angry child. But the truth is I was in fear. I thought that if I continued to fight it would keep people from bothering me. I was really disappointed. I was hurt and it seems that the pain worsened after each traumatic event that had taken place in my life.

I began to recognize that most of the people I loved in my life have been taken from me through the use of violence. In addition, I recognized that my life has been through the cycle of domestic violence. My pain was so agonizing that all I wanted to do was help others so that they wouldn't have to go through the things that I have suffered.

The ambition inside of me began to speak volumes, I recognized that there was more that I had to accomplish other than high school. I knew that if I wanted to make my parents proud and help others, I knew that I had to get a college education. Then, I found out that I had to get a professional license. I turned to educating myself through each traumatic event as far back as I could remember.

I began to understand the stereotypical labels that society has placed on African American males. I decided that I wouldn't be associated with any of the activities that society associated wih that particular group of people. Looking back at my past transgressions, regardless of everything that I've been through, (all the pain, the hurt and the disappointment)... I can say that one of the main things that helped me cope with situation after situation was that my mother didn't allow me to be a victim. She didn't allow me to feel or think that I was different from other kids my age. Yes, I was abused... and I was broken, but she didn't stop chastising me. Nor did she stop punishing me and she give me consequences for behaviors that were not acceptable in her household or in society. I must say that helped me a lot by making me a stronger person.

When I was able to spend time with my father, he taught me how to value relationships with others and to be respectful at all times. He also taught me that life didn't owe me anything and that I had to work for everything I want in life. My father has taught me some of the most valuable lessons in life. One such lesson included telling me the truth even when I was wrong. He never took my side and I knew then that he truly loved me. Love is correction. My father's correction made me a complete person.

I began to understand me, I gained a sense of who I was at that time. I became less angry and more realistic with expectations of myself. I can remember my father telling me that if I ever went to jail, not to make my first call home. What he was saying to me was that he knew that I was smart enough to stay away from situations where I could get in trouble.

When I moved to Mississippi, my grandmother grounded me in the Word of God. She explained what he has done for us. I can always hear her... even in her absence, I hear her saying, "I am so proud of you. I remember when I took you to Bible study and you would talk about God and explained the Word, I was so proud of you punkin'." My grandmother played an instrumental role in my relationship with God. She lead me to the water and I drank it. Even when I didn't want to go, she encouraged me to go anyway. It was my grandmother's love that combatted my confusion of the love from my mother. My grandmother would allow me to build things for her, shell peas, pick greens, and so forth. She taught me how to survive. But, most of all, she taught me that faith without works is dead.

My childhood was not the best but it made me who I am today. As an adult, I have continued to strive for success through love. The pain of my past is the fuel of my motivation to change lives and to make this world a better place. Even the one person who brought me into this world could not break me. I was able to lean on God and it is the love of God that has kept me through everything that I have suffered.

Even though I was going through my trials and tribulations, I could see that light at the end of the tunnel. But somehow, it looked as if the light was moving slow. There was a time in my life when I thought God had forgotten about me, because I couldn't see his words in action. But I knew that life had more to offer and I wanted everything life had to offer. I wanted to prove to myself that I didn't have to conform to stereotypes towards any specific group of minorities. I knew that I was different. I knew that I had no reason to be afraid of showing my intelligence. That is when I truly began to embrace my uniqueness. I began to love me... and as long as I love me I can love others.

Through every obstacle I have faced I have always had the God-given desire to be successful. Regardless of what my parents did or did not do, I was and still am responsible for my own success and to fulfill my God given destiny. Failure is not an option. I was placed in situations' that may have victimized me but I was never a victim. I was born a creator. I learned really fast that God will never put more on me that I can bear. Therefore, "I can do all things through Christ who strengthens me." See, I believe in myself even when others doubt me. My success is not measured by material things but it is measured by the good that I do and the heart that I use to do it with. It is measured by the Love of God to allow me to powerfully connect with children, adolescents and their parents who may need help. Most of all, it is measured by the ability to do it all in and out of love.

RESILIENCE

I Believe in Me.

Clinton C. Patton Sr.

# *About The Author*

RESILIENCE

I Believe in Me.

**Clinton Patton Sr.** is the son of Clinton Hamilton Sr. and Stephanie Patton. He is the CEO at Principles of Resilience Youth Development, LLC., and Patton Behavioral Health, LLC. He received his B.S. in psychology from Texas A&M University - Commerce and a Masters in Human Relations from the University of Oklahoma. He is a Licensed Professional Counselor (LPC) and a man of God. He has been active in the public speaking field for over 8 years specifically in the areas of domestic violence education and intervention, mental health vs. behavioral health, at risk youth empowerment, ways of parenting at risk children and adolescences, bridging the gap between mental health professionals and educators and healthy relationships between mothers and sons.

He has successfully implemented the "Integrated Solutions for Aggression" program at the Principles of Resilience Youth Development, LLC. He has developed an annual workshop specifically for domestic violence intervention, "If I Can't Have You No One Can." His experience includes over 9 years in the mental health field. And he has 8 years of experience as a therapist specializing in various mental health issues such as: depression, ADHD, anxiety, oppositional defiant disorder, PTSD, and so forth.

In addition, he has 7 years of experience in an inpatient facility as a mental health worker, working specifically with sexually abused children. He has worked specifically with families within the lower socio-economic status motivating and facilitating necessary environmental changes conducive for healthy

Clinton C. Patton Sr.

familial functioning.

He is currently establishing the Ashley Renea Hamilton Foundation in order to assist families lacking financial means to obtain mental health services for domestic violence and to provide the opportunity for rebuilding a successful life.

The Foundation came about following the tragic death of Ashley Renea Hamilton. Her death, a result of domestic violence, has sparked a fire inside of Clinton Patton to change the behavioral dynamics contributing to domestic violence, so that families can coexist peacefully within society.

"I believe wholeheartedly that Love is the foundation of success and that love encompasses all things. I believe that in order to get the changes necessary for healthy success is that it is done in and out of love."

Clinton C. Patton Sr. MHR, LPC

# If I Can Succeed... You Can Too!

But I say to you who hear: Love your enemies, do good to those who hate you, bless those who curse you, and pray for those who spitefully use you.

## Luke 6: 27-28

Hey, hey you... reading this book. It is not your fault. I am sorry that you were hurt, but you have to refrain from using your past as a reason for your behavior. This is called the victim mentality and it is not productive. I know that right now it seems like you can't change, but I am here to tell you that you can change. When you change your thoughts you change your life. I challenge you to think positive, to change your environment and to forgive yourself because you are worthy of Love. You are unique and should embrace your differences. Do not be afraid to display that you are intelligent.

Admit your faults. You have to take responsibility for your actions by admitting what you did and choose not to engage in the same behavior. Focus your negative energy towards something positive. Do things that you are good at. Love yourself unconditionally. There is no fear in love for perfect love casts out all fear, never be afraid to succeed. Learn from your mistakes but don't beat yourself up. We all make mistakes and you are not alone.

Respect your parents and any other adult, because one day you will become an adult. Keep in mind that you do not have to time

Clinton C. Patton Sr.

change, change is a daily process. It is your destiny to be great - you have everything you need to be successful. You have to look within and bring out your internal drive. No one can stop you from being successful, you can choose to be great or you can choose to be mediocre. Nothing is impossible. Never let anyone make you think or feel that you are inadequate, you are enough. Keep in mind that you have to love yourself before you can recognize love, accept love and be loved. Believe that you have a purpose and that purpose is to be successful.

I have made bad choices. One time, my classmate and I decided to make a prank call to 911 from our school. We picked up the phone, dialed 911 and stated, "My baby is choking on a chicken bone!" We hung up the phone, then we went back to the library as if nothing happened. Soon after that the police showed up at our school and asked who were the last people to leave the library. We were thinking that we would get away with it, but the librarian had other plans. He told the police that it was us. They put each of our hands in handcuffs and escorted us to the police station. They made our parents come pick us up.  When you make a choice that has negative consequences try not to allow your response to be "I am not perfect," because that is an excuse to make the same mistake over again. Besides, that goes without saying. You have the capacity to learn therefore your future can be whatever you want it to be. Your past doesn't have to define you, your present or your future, you can live in the present and move towards your successful future.  If I can turn my past into my fuel to succeed then anyone can. Jfust believe in you. I believe in you!

# You are Awesome!

Through the village that I was raised in, I learned what I needed as a male child to become successful.

# *Affirmations of Love*

"Love encompasses ALL things."

I am love

I am patient

I do not boast or brag

I do not rejoice in iniquity

I have not fear, I have love

I am extraordinary

I love my self

I am courageous

I am smart

I am intelligent

I love to help people

I am kind

I believe in love

I am loyal

I am unique

I am educated

I am an overcomer

I love myself

I don't have to use violence to get my needs met

I am peaceful

I am positive

I am loved

I am caring

I am resilient

I am a conqueror

"Repeat aloud or mentally until you can believe in yourself"

Clinton C. Patton Sr.

# Things to Remember

- Words hurt
- Pain causes pain
- I am strengthened by my relationship with God
- I have learned to say I love you and I have learned to act out of love
- Through every traumatic event, I turned to education
- Education is the foundation for success
- VIOLENCE is never a good choice, keep your hands and feet to yourself
- Nobody wins in a fight
- Do everything out of LOVE, LOVE encompasses all things
- The first characteristic of a man or woman is love
- Violence does not contain love
- You will never get anything good out of doing bad things
- Love doesn't manipulate and loving yourself does not manipulate others
- I am no different from you, if I can make it through everything that I have been through, you can too.
- I am here to tell you that you can too!
- Listening will save your life
- Anger is a secondary emotion.
- Your ENVIRONMENT does not necessarily mean the physical surroundings,
- You have to change your mental environment in order to change your life.
- Treat others how you would want to be treated.

Clinton C. Patton Sr.

- Birds of the same feather flock together.

- You do not have time, you should take every second, every minute, every hour to make steps towards change, you need to change and the time is now.

- Doing the same thing and expecting different results, is the definition of insanity.

# *Personal Development*

## WORKBOOKS

Eat honey, dear child—it's good for you
and delicacies that melt in your mouth.
Likewise knowledge,
and wisdom for your soul—Get that and your future's
secured, your hope in on solid rock.

**Proverbs 24:13 -14**

Clinton C. Patton Sr.

## Stereotypes of Minorities
Stereotypes can hurt you and develop your personal expectations.

## Who Am I?
Positive traits and self-esteem

## Ticking Time Bomb
Triggers, alternatives and resuts

## Physical Aggression
Get to the core of your physical aggression.

## Emotional/Psychological Abuse
Define, acknowledge and overcome

## Master of Manipulation
How manipulation hurts you and others

## I Didn't Do Anything
The difference between being a victim and living life as a victim.

## What is Love?
Identifying true love.

## The Book of Instruction
Scriptures you can lean on.

## Act Like a Man/Woman
Maturity and spirituality

## Accepting Rejection
The word "No" and the power you give it.

## Where is My Ambition?
Passion, purpose and pain.

## Forgiveness is Freedom
Forgiving yourself and others

## Healthy Relationships
Creating, recognizing and maintaining healthy relationships

## How to Be a Friend
Identifying the core characteristics of being a friend.

# RESILIENCE
I Believe in Me.

Clinton C. Patton Sr.

# *Stereotypes of Minorities*

Stereotypes can hurt you and develop your personal expectations.

## Instructions:

Place your first and last name in the blanks and repeat each sentence aloud with confidence.

(In order to defeat any stereotype you have to know what they are, and work twice as hard to refrain from stereotypical behaviors.)

1. _____

   is not in prison or jail.

2. _____

   is educated.

3. _____

   is not a part of a gang.

4. _____

   does not sell drugs.

5. _____

   is not violent or aggressive.

6. _____

   is not ignorant.

7. _____

   is not a mistake.

Clinton C. Patton Sr.

**Instructions:** Write About Your Experience with Stereotypes

_____

_____

_____

_____

_____

_____

_____

_____

_____

_____

_____

_____

_____

_____

_____

_____

_____

_____

_____

_____

_____

_____

_____

_____

Clinton C. Patton Sr.

RESILIENCE

## **Stereotypes of Minorities**

### 5 Points to Remember

**1.** Stay away from situations that may lead to jail or prison.

**2.** Stay in school, make good grades.

**3.** Stay away from gangs.

**4.** Think before you act.

**5.** Study to acquire knowledge. Knowledge IS Power.

# Who Am I?

Positive traits and self-esteem

## Instructions:

Complete the following questions.

Name 6 positive traits about you.

1. _____
2. _____
3. _____
4. _____
5. _____
6. _____

What does Self Esteem mean to you?

_____

_____

_____

What does Self Esteem look like (High/Low)

_____

_____

_____

_____

RESILIENCE

I Believe in Me.

Clinton C. Patton Sr.

**Instructions:** Write About An Experience with Self-Esteem

Clinton C. Patton Sr.

RESILIENCE

## Who Am I?

### 5 Points to Remember

**1.** Think positive to obtain positive results.

**2.** Maintain good hygiene, when you look good you feel good.

**3.** Love yourself at all times.

**4.** Replace negative thoughts with positive thoughts.

**5.** Focus on things that you do well, things you are good at.

# Ticking Time Bomb

Triggers, alternatives and resuts

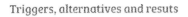

## Instructions:

Complete the following items below.

What are your triggers for anger?

_____

_____

_____

_____

_____

How does your anger effect your loved ones (family& friends)?

_____

_____

What are alternatives for your anger (What can you do, other that becoming angry)?

_____

_____

_____

Clinton C. Patton Sr.

**Instructions:** Write About Your Experience with Anger

_____

_____

_____

_____

_____

_____

_____

_____

_____

_____

_____

_____

_____

_____

_____

_____

_____

_____

_____

_____

_____

_____

_____

_____

# RESILIENCE

## **Ticking Time Bomb**

### 6 Points to Remember

**1.** Talk about your feelings wth someone you trust.

**2.** Think about how your anger impacts your family and changes your behavior.

**3.** Use your coping skills when you recognize triggers for anger.

**4.** Think before you speak. "Will what I am about to say hurt others?"

**5.** If you don't have anything nice to say, don't say it at all.

**6.** When you say mean things, you CAN'T take them back and sorry doesn't fix it.

# Physical Aggression

Get to the core of your physical aggression.

## Instructions:

Complete the following items below.

Name any time where you have used physical aggression?

_____

_____

_____

_____

How does physical aggression effect friendships with others?

_____

_____

What can you do other physical aggression to resolve conflict?

_____

_____

_____

**Instructions:** Write About Your Experience with Physical Aggression

_____

_____

_____

_____

_____

_____

_____

_____

_____

_____

_____

_____

_____

_____

_____

_____

_____

_____

_____

_____

_____

_____

_____

_____

Clinton C. Patton Sr.

# Physical Aggression

## 4 Points to Remember

**1.** Keep your hands and feet to yourself.

**2.** Put yourself in someone else's shoes as if someone was aggressive toward you.

**3.** Walk away when you feel that physical aggression may occur.

**4.** Use your words, talk out your problems.

# Emotional/ Psychological Abuse

**Get to the core of your physical aggression.**

## Instructions:

Complete the following items below.

What is emotional/ psychological abuse?

_____

_____

What are the effects of emotional/
psychological abuse?

_____

_____

Name a time where you have been
emotionally abused, and how did you feel
during the process?

_____

_____

Name a time where you have been
emotionally abusive towards someone,
how did you feel during the process?

_____

_____

What are alternatives to use instead of
emotional abuse?

_____

_____

Clinton C. Patton Sr.

**Fill in the Blank.**

_____ and _____
[are] in the power of the tongue: and they that love it shall eat the fruit
thereof.

Proverbs 18:21

There is that _____ like the piercings of a sword: but the
_____ of the wise [is] health.

Proverbs 12: 13

Whoso _____ his mouth and his tongue
_____ his soul from troubles.

Proverbs 21: 23

**Instructions:** Journal any Emotional/Psychological Abuse

_____

_____

_____

_____

_____

_____

_____

_____

_____

_____

_____

_____

_____

_____

_____

_____

_____

_____

_____

_____

_____

_____

_____

_____

# Emotional/Psychological Abuse

## 6 Points to Remember

**1.** Don't use profanity when you speak with others.

**2.** Don't name call, it makes people feel bad about themselves.

**3.** Refrain from condescending behaviors toward others.

**4.** Give compliments, say nice things.

**5.** Be patient with others.

**6.** Treat each other how you want to be treated at all times.

# Master of Manipulation

## Instructions:

Complete the following items below.

What is manipulation?

_____

_____

How have you been manipulative?

_____

_____

How has your manipulative ways affected others?

_____

_____

What can you do other than manipulate others to get what you need and/or want?

_____

_____

How do your thoughts encourage the way you behave?

_____

_____

Compare and contrast manipulation and selfishness.

_____

_____

Clinton C. Patton Sr.

**Instructions:** Write About Your Experience with Manipulation

# RESILIENCE

## Master of Manipulation

### 5 Points to Remember

**1.** Be honest abou what you need or want in the beginning.

**2.** Manipulation hurts other people.

**3.** Manipulation is deceitful and places others in negative situations.

**4.** There is no manipulation in love.

**5.** Manipulation often leads to abuse.

# *I Didn't Do Anything...*

**Playing the Victim**

## Instructions:

Complete the following items below.

What is the victim mentality?

_____

_____

What is the difference between being
victimized and the victim mentality?

_____

_____

Have you experienced the victim mentality?
Or played the victim?

_____

_____

What does the world owe you?

_____

_____

What ways can you stop playing the victim,
and can you become successful by playing the
victim? Explain.

_____

_____

_____

Clinton C. Patton Sr.

**Instructions:** Write About Your Experience with Denial

## RESILIENCE

# I Didn't Do Anything

### 5 Points to Remember

**1.** Take responsibility for your actions by admitting your mistake and don't do it again.

**2.** The world doesn't owe you anything, you owe it to yourself to be resilient.

**3.** Stop blaming others for your behavior, you were not forced to do anything.

**4.** Stop playing the victim by accepting your part... what did you do?

**5.** Be honest with yourself if you made a mistake.

# *What is Love?*

## Instructions:

### Complete the following items below.

Place the appropiate words from scripture into the blanks below.

_____ suffers long and is kind; _____ does not envy; _____ does not parade itself, is not puffed up; _____ does not behave rudely, does not seek its own, _____ is not provoked, _____ thinks no evil; _____ does not rejoice in iniquity, but rejoices in the truth; 7 bears all things, believes all things, hopes all things, endures all things.
*1 Corinthians 13:4-5*

I will praise You, for I am _____ and _____ made; marvelous are your works, and that my soul knows very well.
*Psalms 134:14 NKJV*

"When I was a child, I spoke as a child, I understood as a child, I thought as a child; but when I became a man, I put away childish things."
*1 Corinthians 13:11 NKJV*

For God so _____ the world, that he _____ his only begotten Son, that whosoever believeth in him should not perish, but have everlasting life.

For God _____ not his Son into the world to condemn the world; but that the world through him might be

_____ .

*John 3: 16-17 NKJV*

Clinton C. Patton Sr.

**Instructions:** Write About Your Experience with Love

# What is Love?

## 5 Points to Remember

**1.** Do and say things out of love, love is correction.

**2.** Look in the mirror and recite, 'I love myself' daily until you start to believe it.

**3.** God is love and you were made in God's image so that means that you are love.

**4.** Love encompasses all things.

**5.** He that spareth his rod hateth his son: but he that loveth him chasen

# The Book of Instruction

**Instructions:**

Complete the following items below.

Place the appropiate words from scripture into the blanks below.

1) _____ loves instruction loves knowledge, But he who hates correction is _____ .
*Proverbs 12:1*

2) There is no _____ in love; but perfect _____ casts out fear, because _____ involves torment. But he who _____ has not been made perfect in _____ ."
*I John 4:18*

3) _____ and _____ are in the power of the tongue,

And those who _____ it will eat its fruit.
*Proverbs 18:21*

4) The _____ of the _____ uses knowledge rightly, But the mouth of _____ pours forth _____ .

*Proverbs 15:2*

Why is it important to have rules?

_____

_____

_____

_____

_____

How do you feel when you are given instructions?

_____

_____

_____

_____

_____

Describe the world without rules, would you feel safe?

_____

_____

_____

_____

_____

"My son, hear the instruction of thy father, and forsake not the law of thy mother:"

_Proverbs 1:8_

**Instructions:** Write what you know about The Book of Instruction

_____

_____

_____

_____

_____

_____

_____

_____

_____

_____

_____

_____

_____

_____

_____

_____

_____

_____

_____

_____

_____

_____

_____

_____

_____

Clinton C. Patton Sr.

RESILIENCE

# The Book of Instruction
### 6 Points to Remember

**1.** Love is correction.

**2.** When making decisions always think about how your consequences will affect your family.

**3.** Be quiet when someone is talking to you, it is extremely difficult to listen and talk at the same time.

**4.** Follow instructions it is for your own protection.

**5.** Ask questions in a respectful manner if you don't understand what is asked of you.

**6.** Listening will save your life.

# *Act Like a Man*

## Instructions:

Complete the following items below.

What does it mean to be a man?

_____

_____

_____

_____

What does it mean to be a male child?

_____

_____

_____

_____

**Fill in the Blank.**

Be _____ and of a
good _____,
_____ not, nor be
_____ of them: for the LORD
thy God, he [it is] that doth go with thee; he
will not fail thee, nor forsake thee.

*Deuteronomy 31:6*

A man shall not be established by
_____ : but the root of the
righteous shall not be moved.

*Proverbs 12:3*

RESILIENCE

I Believe in Me.

Clinton C. Patton Sr.

**Instructions:** Write About the Type of Man You Would Like to Be

Clinton C. Patton Sr.

**RESILIENCE**

## Act Like a Man

### 5 Points to Remember

**1.** Don't be afraid to show that you are intelligent.

**2.** Don't be afraid to show love, it has nothing to do with your masculinity.

**3.** Don't argue with women, men don't argue.

**4.** Stand up for yourself when others are engaging in negative behaviors.

**5.** Put away your childish ways, be mature.

# *Act Like a Woman*

## Instructions:

Complete the following items below.

What does it mean to be a woman?

_____

_____

_____

What does it mean to be a female child?

_____

_____

_____

Who can find a virtuous woman? For her price is far above _____ .

The heart of her husband doth safely trust in her, so that he shall have no need of spoil.

She will do him _____ and not _____ all the days of her life.

She seeketh wool, and flax, and worketh willingly with her hands.

She is like the merchants' ships; she bringeth her food from afar.

She riseth also while it is yet night, and giveth meat to her household, and a portion to her maidens.

She considereth a field, and buyeth it: with the fruit of her hands she planteth a vineyard.

She girdeth her loins with strength, and _____ her arms.

She perceiveth that her merchandise is

## RESILIENCE

I Believe in Me.

good: her candle goeth not out by night.

She _____ her hands to the spindle, and her hands hold the distaff.

She _____ out her hand to the poor; yea, she reacheth forth her hands to the needy.

She is not afraid of the snow for her household: for all her household are clothed with _____.

She maketh herself coverings of tapestry; her clothing is silk and purple.

Her husband is known in the gates, when he sitteth among the elders of the land.

She _____ fine linen, and selleth it; and delivereth girdles unto the merchant.

Strength and honour are her clothing; and she shall rejoice in time to come.

She _____her mouth with wisdom; and in her tongue is the _____ of _____.

She _____ well to the ways of her household, and _____ not the bread of idleness.

Her children arise up, and call her _____; her husband also, and he praiseth her.

Many daughters have done virtuously, but thou excellest them all.

Favour is deceitful, and beauty is vain: but a woman that feareth the LORD, she shall be _____.

Give her of the fruit of her hands; and let her own works praise her in the gates.

Proverbs 31:10-31

**Instructions:** Write About the Type of Woman You Would Like to Be

_____

_____

_____

_____

_____

_____

_____

_____

_____

_____

_____

_____

_____

_____

_____

_____

_____

_____

_____

_____

_____

_____

Clinton C. Patton Sr.

RESILIENCE

## Act Like a Woman
### 5 Points to Remember

**1.** Think before you speak, your words can hurt, belittle and degrade.

**2.** Motivate others to be successful.

**3.** If you do not have anything nice to say, don't say it at all.

**4.** Be kind even through trials and tribulations.

**5.** Lead with your heart, think about it and make a good decision.

## Accepting Rejection

### Instructions:

Complete the following items below.

What is rejection?

_____

_____

_____

_____

When you are told "NO," what do think at that moment and why?

_____

_____

_____

As you come to him, a living stone
_____ by
men but in the sight of God chosen and
precious

*1 Peter 2:4*

"The one who hears you hears me, and the
one who _____ you rejects me,
and the one who _____ me
_____ him who sent me."

*Luke 10:16*

*"No, does not place you in a grave or prison,
but it does place boundaries where they are
needed"*

-Clinton Patton Sr. MHR. LPC.-

Clinton C. Patton Sr.

**Instructions:** Write About Your Experience with Rejection

_____

_____

_____

_____

_____

_____

_____

_____

_____

_____

_____

_____

_____

_____

_____

_____

_____

_____

_____

_____

_____

_____

_____

_____

_____

Clinton C. Patton Sr.

# Accepting Rejection
## 5 Points to Remember

**1.** "No" is not the end of the world.

**2.** "No" does not mean that you are a bad person or no one loves you.

**3.** Tell yourself "no" sometimes it's good for you.

**4.** When you feel like you are being rejected, think about 3 positive reasons why people like you.

# Where is My Ambition?

## Instructions:

Complete the following items below.

What are you passionate about?

_____

_____

_____

_____

Who are you passionate about?

_____

_____

_____

What would you change about the world
and why?

_____

_____

_____

What would you tell a child who is going
through similar situations as those that you
have experienced?

_____

_____

_____

_____

Clinton C. Patton Sr.

What is unique about you; something you would want people to know, and you haven't told anyone?

_____

_____

_____

_____

_____

_____

_____

_____

_____

_____

**Fill in the blank.**

Therefore if there is any consolation in Christ, if any comfort of _____, if any fellowship of the _____, if any affection and mercy, fulfill my joy by being like-minded, having the same love, being of one accord, of one mind. Let _____ be done through selfish _____ or conceit, but in _____ of mind let each esteem others better than himself. Let each of you look out not only for his own interests, but also for the interests of others.

*2 Philippians 2:1-4*

**Instructions:** Write About Your Ambitions

_____

_____

_____

_____

_____

_____

_____

_____

_____

_____

_____

_____

_____

_____

_____

_____

_____

_____

_____

_____

_____

_____

_____

_____

## Where is My Ambition?

### 4 Points to Remember

**1.** Focus on things that you are passionate about.

**2.** Think of ways that you can make this world a better place.

**3.** Think outside the box.

**4.** Write your ideas down and then put your ideas into action one day at a time.

# *Forgiveness is Freedom*

## Instructions:

Complete the following items below.

*Keep in mind that in order to forgive others who may have hurt you, you must learn to forgive yourself.*

What is forgiveness?

_____

_____

_____

_____

What does it mean to forgive yourself?

_____

_____

_____

_____

In what ways can you forgive others who have hurt you?

_____

_____

_____

_____

Why is it important to forgive yourself and others?

_____

_____

_____

_____

Clinton C. Patton Sr.

What are physical and emotional problems that can be associated with not forgiving others?

_____

_____

_____

_____

What does it mean to be vengeful, or to get revenge?

_____

_____

_____

_____

How does vengeance or getting revenge help you?

_____

_____

_____

_____

How would you feel if someone was to seek vengeance or get revenge on you?

_____

_____

_____

_____

What can you do other than vengeance or seeking revenge to solve conflicts with others?

_____

_____

_____

_____

**Write the "Golden Rule"**

_____

Be _____ to one another, tenderhearted,
_____ one another, as God in Christ
forgave you.

*Ephesians 4:32*

_____ not, and ye shall not be judged:
condemn not, and ye shall not be condemned: _____ , and
ye shall be _____ :

*Luke 6: 37*

**Instructions:** Write About an Experience with Forgiveness

Clinton C. Patton Sr.

## RESILIENCE

# **Forgiveness is Freedom**
## 5 Points to Remember

**1.** Forgive yourself for whatever it is that you have done, it's time to move forward.

**2.** Lack of forgiveness is painful physically and mentally for you.

**3.** Don't seek revenge.

**4.** Forgiveness is as if it never happened.

**5.** Treat others how you want to be treated.

# Healthy Relationships

**Instructions:**

Complete the following items below.

What does a healthy relationship look like?

_____

_____

_____

_____

What are positive characteristics of a
healthy relationship?

_____

_____

_____

_____

What does "Birds of a feather flock
together" mean?

_____

_____

_____

_____

What can you do to create healthy
relationships with others?

_____

_____

_____

_____

RESILIENCE

I Believe in Me.

Clinton C. Patton Sr.

**Fill in the blank.**

For the whole law is fulfilled in one word: "You shall _____
your neighbor as yourself."

*Galatians 5:14*

**Instructions:** Write About a Healthy Relationship

_____

_____

_____

_____

_____

_____

_____

_____

_____

_____

_____

_____

_____

_____

_____

_____

_____

_____

_____

_____

_____

_____

_____

_____

_____

## RESILIENCE

# Healthy Relationships
### 6 Points to Remember

**1.** Attitude is very important, be mindful of how you say things.

**2.** Disagreements are not arguments.

**3.** Focus on positive things within your relationship.

**4.** Love encompasses all things and is unconditional.

**5.** Be committed to maintaining a healthy relationship.

**6.** Life and death lies within the tongue, be careful what you say... it has a way of seeping into the atmosphere.

# How to Be a Friend

## Instructions:

Complete the following items below.

What characteristics should you have in order to be a good friend?

_____
_____
_____
_____

What characteristics should someone you consider a friend have?

_____
_____
_____
_____

What does it mean to have social skills?

_____
_____
_____
_____

Why is it important to be a friend to others?

_____
_____
_____
_____
_____

Clinton C. Patton Sr.

Fill in the blank.....

A man of many companions may come to ruin, but there is a
_____ who sticks closer than a brother.

*Proverbs 18:24*


Two are better than _____, because they have a good
reward for their toil. For if they _____, one will lift up his
fellow. But woe to him who is alone when he falls and has not another
to _____ him up! Again, if two lie _____, they
keep warm, but how can one keep warm alone? And though a man
might prevail against one who is alone, two will withstand him—a
threefold cord is not quickly broken.

*Ecclesiastes 4:9-12*


A_____ loves at all times, and a _____ is born
for adversity.

*Proverbs 17:17*

**Instructions:** Write About a How to Be a Friend

_____

_____

_____

_____

_____

_____

_____

_____

_____

_____

_____

_____

_____

_____

_____

_____

_____

_____

_____

_____

_____

_____

_____

_____

Clinton C. Patton Sr.

**RESILIENCE**

# How to Be a Friend

## 6 Points to Remember

**1.** Be completely honest even if you are afraid of losing a friend.

**2.** Friends tell you the truth even if you don't like it.

**3.** Encourage others to do the right thing.

**4.** Ask yourself would you be your own friend and make the changes needed.

**5.** Show interest as it pertains to differences. Friendships require comprising sometimes as well.

**6.** Be the friend that you want to have as a friend.

*When you feel like there is no hope,
write it down in the journal provided,
release your pain, look at my pain and know
that it will be over soon.*

_____

_____

_____

_____

_____

_____

_____

_____

_____

_____

_____

_____

_____

_____

_____

_____

_____

_____

_____

_____

_____

_____

Clinton C. Patton Sr.

Clinton C. Patton Sr.

Clinton C. Patton Sr.

Clinton C. Patton Sr.

Clinton C. Patton Sr.

Clinton C. Patton Sr.

Clinton C. Patton Sr.

_____
_____
_____
_____
_____
_____
_____
_____
_____
_____
_____
_____
_____
_____
_____
_____
_____
_____
_____
_____
_____
_____
_____
_____

Clinton C. Patton Sr.

# Sketch It

## "Your past does not have to be your present "

*When I was going through trying times, I found that drawing took me to another place. I would also color what I drew, it helped me to cope with my pain and it helped me to increase my self-esteem because it was something that I practiced a lot until I became good at it, so I have provided a sketch pad, try it, it may take you to places you have never imagined.*

Clinton C. Patton Sr.

Clinton C. Patton Sr.

Clinton C. Patton Sr.

Clinton C. Patton Sr.

Clinton C. Patton Sr.

Clinton C. Patton Sr.

Clinton C. Patton Sr.

Ashley R. Hamilton

Stanley Patton

Larry Patton

Charles Patton Sr.

Oliver Ricky Hamilton

Lee Willie Hamilton Sr.

John Yates III

Link White

Kendrick White

Ernest Patton Sr.

Rosie White

Rose Patton

Omar Patton

Azallene Morris

## "Correction is All Out of Love."

-Clinton C. Patton Sr. MHR, LPC-